This Me

A prayer Warriors Journa

This Means War

A Prayer Warrior Journal for healing and deliverance...

I would first like to thank my personal Lord and Savior Jesus Christ; it's because of God that I am who I am. I would like to thank my Family and friends who has stuck by me no matter what. I like to thank God for my Church Faith Christian worship Center under the leadership of my Pastor and friend Rev. Gary G Johnson Sr. And my First Lady Naomi Johnson
Specifically I'd like to thank God for my Husband Thomas, my children Lawrence, Dayna, Tommy Jr, Amoni, Jamarr, and Jordan. My Mother Juanita, my siblings, especially Stacy, Wanda, and Larry as well as my nieces, nephews. I would also like to thank everyone that has prayed and encouraged me especially Dedra, for all of your love and Support in my life. I love you all more than you will ever know.

God gave me a vision to write this devotional in 2016, I struggled writing this for years. I knew that it wouldn't be easy; when ever healing and deliverance is involved the enemy will always work overtime...
In this devotional you will experience a lot of my life and some of yours. It's time for us to take back our lives and I mean every part of it. In this devotional you will realize that you don't have to allow your past or your current situation to dictate your worth or your life. As you read in the title [THIS MEANS WAR]
So put on your armor and get ready for healing and deliverance.

Contents

Dedication

I would like to dedicate this book to my Mother Juanita Robinson, Amazing mother, grandmother, sister, aunt, and friend. I am who I am because God blessed me with such an amazing woman to not only birth me but raise me. My mother passed away July 2020 after a lengthy illness, and this turned my whole life around. This special woman was my biggest supporter, best friend, and the most loved person that I have ever met. Mommy I know that you are smiling down on me and covering as you are now my special angle. I love and miss you with everything within me. You will always be a major part of our lives.

Prayer Journal

Generational Curses!!!

Exodus 34:7: I Lavish unfailing love to a thousand generations, I forgive iniquity, rebellion, and sin. But I do not excuse the guilty. I lay the sins of the parents upon their children and grandchildren; the entire family is affected even children in the third and fourth generations.

I want to talk a little bit about generational curses and our children. We as parents have a duty to raise our children to be the best humans that they can be. In this society it's not easy. It's not easy for several reasons. The first and second reason is that we don't always know how to raise them to be great, especially if we don't love our selves. Thirdly if we don't recognize these generational curses we can't help them. Most importantly if we don't have a relationship and a connection with God we will never understand the seriousness of this matter. Generational curses can be so many things, like lying, cheating, depression, low self worth, poor money management, drug addiction, alcohol addiction just to name a few. If we want to make sure that these curses don't attach themselves to our children it's time to connect and put on the full armor of God.

Ephesians 6:10-17 "Finally, be strong in the Lord and in his mighty power. Put on the full armor of God, so that you can take your stand against the devil's schemes. For our struggle is not against flesh and blood, but against the rulers, against the authorities, against the powers of this dark world and against the spiritual forces of evil in the heavenly realms. Therefore put on the full armor of God, so that when the day of evil comes, you may be able to stand your ground, and after you have done everything, to stand. Stand firm then, with the belt of truth buckled around your waist, with the breastplate of righteousness in place, and with your feet fitted with the readiness that comes from the gospel of peace. In addition to all this, take up the shield of faith, with which you can extinguish all the flaming arrows of the evil one. Take the helmet of salvation and the sword of the Spirit, which is the word of God."

We have to realize that the enemy is real and of course he does not want to see our youth to become great. Guess what beloved the enemy doesn't have the final say. One thing that I want to let you know is that any positive seed can break any barrier...

Most Holy and all wise God I come thanking you praising you and giving your name all the glory God I come against any and every generational curse that lay dormant upon our young people I come against the spirit of depression, low self esteem, low self worth, homosexuality, drug addiction alcohol abuse, bullying, every and anything that the enemy will try to attach to our children. I come against it in the name of Jesus I pray for favor upon our children, Galatians 5:1 it is for freedom that Christ has set us free. Stand firm, then, and do not let yourselves be burdened again by a yoke of slavery. Have your way in and through their lives touch them in such an amazing way guide them use them wrap them in your arms have your way in their lives that you will be glorified in the enemy will be horrified I thank you in advance for your healing power in Jesus name I pray Amen Amen and Amen!!!

Prayer Journal

_____

_____

_____

_____

_____

_____

_____

_____

_____

_____

_____

_____

_____

_____

_____

_____

_____

_____

_____

_____

_____

You're as sick as your secrets...

Mark 4:22 For everything that is hidden will eventually be brought into the open, and every secret will be brought to light.

Back in the day families would say that whatever happens in this house stays in this house... Let me just tell you that if you are being abused in any way you should open your mouth. There are so many dysfunctional families in this world because of this mentality. Have you ever heard of the saying you're as sick as your secrets? There is so much truth in that statement, do you know how much healing that can take place if we would just open our mouths. You/We must stop being held in bondage because society says so. This is a new season for us all. Family in this day and age it seems as if everything is acceptable. Let's take a hold of our families and refuse to allow the enemy or society to control our actions.

Most humble and all wise God we need you, it seems as if this world is going to hell in a hand basket. Father we know that if we but touch the hem of your garment we will be made well. Mentally, physically and emotionally. Show up God; help us to do what needs to be done. Fall fresh over every person that may be dealing with secrets that will ultimately cause them to fall, every secret that will have us doing things that's out of our character, every secret that will cause us to hurt one another. Lord let it start in the church house and trickle down to the nation. God we are helpless without you and can do nothing without you. Help us Lord!!!! We need you right now, snatch us out of darkness and allow us to seek and trust you with every part of us. Place your healing hands all over us in Jesus name Amen Amen and Amen!!!

Prayer Journal

_____

_____

_____

_____

_____

_____

_____

_____

_____

_____

_____

_____

_____

_____

_____

_____

_____

_____

Protecting your children...

Matthew 18:6 But whoever causes one of these little ones who believe in me to sin, it would be better for him to have a millstone fastened around his neck and to be drowned in the depth of the sea.

Children are a gift and should be treated as such. When the Lord blesses you with the gift of having a child or children you should cherish them more than you cherish a material gift. When God entrusted them to you He expects for you to love, nurture, care for and protect them. You're child/children should always feel safe and loved by and with you. Children are jewels, you wouldn't treat your valuables any kind of way, and you shouldn't treat your children any kind of way. If a child can't feel safe with their parents no telling who they will trust their safety to. Parents be there for your children, they need you more than you know. If you ask a lot of children that are in juvenile detention centers or jail how was their relationship with their parents. They will tell you that they never felt the love or support from their parents. That's why it's very important that you love your children and keep them grounded in church. At least in church you have a village to help you raise them. It's a most to encourage and show love and kindness to children. Just know that you are their first love and you set the atmosphere on how they will allow people to treat them. It's okay to tell them that you love them and hug on them, let them know that they are a blessing to you.

Most humble and all wise God I come praying for our youth and the love or the lack of love that they are being shown by their parents or caregivers. Lord wrap them in your loving arms. Comfort them as only you can. Let them know how special they are to you. Speak to the parents and teach them how to parent, how to love, how to nurture, and how to care for them. Jesus be a fence all around them. Lord I speak life over every young person that's seeking attention from a parent; I come against that spirit that will cause them to go astray. I come against that spirit that will cause them to settle. I come against that spirit that will cause them to look for love in all the wrong places. Meet them at their very need and remove generational curses that will cause them to continue these cycles and past them down to future generations in Jesus name I pray Amen Amen and Amen!!!

Prayer Journal

_____

_____

_____

_____

_____

_____

_____

_____

_____

_____

_____

_____

_____

_____

_____

_____

_____

_____

Fighting to keep your peace!!!

Romans 5:1 Therefore, since we have been justified by Faith, we have peace with God through our Lord Jesus Christ.

There are times when life and the people in it will try to steal your peace. If we are not careful they or it will steal your peace right from under you. It could be people or situations, remember beloved life comes at you fast and things will happen suddenly. Be strong and fight for your peace, don't allow the world or the people in it to suck you up. God is your keeper and a very present help... hold on to His unchanging hand. Put and keep God first day in and day out. Sometimes the enemy will use the people you love the most to break you, so we must stay woke. These are some examples of how to keep God first. Give Him your first fruit of the day, such as praying first thing in the morning, pray before you get your day started, and journal. We must focus on the Prince of Peace, He will always win!!!

Most humble and all wise God I come praying for peace, Lord I ask that you would rebuild everything that was stolen from each person reading this. God you said in your word that you would never put more on us than we could bare, sometimes life becomes very hard and we can't see a way of escape. Lord we need to see what it is that you see in us and what it is that you require from us, so that we can live a life that is pleasing to you. God I know that you are a very present help so we are asking for your HELP in this situation. I know that we can do all things but fail as long as we have you with us, but sometimes we feel so alone. God please come and see about us.... I know that we are not perfect but we serve a perfect God! Lord we need you right now. Have your way oh mighty King have your way! Amen Amen and Amen!!!

Prayer Journal

_____

_____

_____

_____

_____

_____

_____

_____

_____

_____

_____

_____

_____

_____

_____

_____

_____

Marriage!!!

Ephesians 5:21-28 "And further, submit to one another out of reverence for Christ. For wives, this means submit to your husbands as to the Lord. For a husband is the head of his wife as Christ is the head of the church. He is the Savior of his body, the church. As the church submits to Christ, so you wives should submit to your husbands in everything. For husbands, this means love your wives, just as Christ loved the church. He gave up his life for her to make her holy and clean, washed by the cleansing of God's word. He did this to present her to himself as a glorious church without a spot or wrinkle or any other blemish. Instead, she will be holy and without fault. In the same way, husbands ought to love their wives as they love their own bodies. For a man who loves his wife actually shows love for himself."

Who ever told you that marriage is easy they lied. There is nothing easy about marriage; you have your good days and bad days. Sometimes you may have more good than bad and there will be times when you have more bad than good. It's all up to you! First of all God has to be the center. Without God you are just living, and that doesn't mean you are living good. You have two different personalities and then once you have a child that's another ball game. Would I trade being married for a single life no, who would unless it's an unhealthy one? I believe that the enemy will always try to attack marriages, why because he knows how precious marriage is to God.
Genesis 2:24 "Therefore a man shall leave his father and his mother and hold fast to his wife, and they shall become one."

When two people decide to commit to being with each other for the rest of their lives the enemy will surely try his unholy hand. We have to look at our relationship like a gift from God and cherish it. No you won't always see eye to eye but if God is in it there should be no limit. There are some keys to having a successful and powerful marriage.
1: Allow God to be the center... Pray together
2: Respect each other… Never talk down to one another
3: Love each other… Express your feelings to each other never hide your feelings
With these things your marriage won't be perfect but it will be blessed.

All Wise Father I come praying for marriages everywhere, I pray for favor and blessing over every married couple that may be going through. Lord I ask that you would bring back to their remembrance the love that was once shared between the two. Lord I ask that you would be that third strand. God I know that a three strand cord is not easily broken. God have your way. Father there are too many married saints suffering and struggling. Lord show up as only you can. Breathe life back into each marriage and relationship. Bring respect and unconditional love back to them. Allow each person to remember the vows that were taken, and show them everything that they fell in love with so that marriages will last and be blessed... Show up God in Jesus name Amen Amen and Amen!!!

Prayer Journal

_____

_____

_____

_____

_____

_____

_____

_____

_____

_____

_____

_____

_____

_____

_____

_____

_____

How Easy Is It To Love Yourself???

Psalm 139:13-15 "You made all the delicate, inner parts of my body and knit me together in my mother's womb. Thank you for making me so wonderfully complex! Your workmanship is marvelous—how well I know it. You watched me as I was being formed in utter seclusion, as I was woven together in the dark of the womb."

As much as we may think that this is an easy task, it can be one of the hardest things in the world to love you. Sometimes we have to ask ourselves do I love me? When you look in the mirror do you see love? When you talk about you do you feel love? Do you criticize yourself more than others? Do you get defensive when others see flaws? In this season let's focus on loving ourselves; it's time to stop putting everyone and everything in front of your happiness. I know that it can be the hardest thing to do especially when you've been a wife, mother, and sometimes the glue that holds everyone together for so long. It has come to a point where you don't even know how to take care of you. Ask yourself what good am I to everyone else if I'm not here for me? There are so many ways that you can take care of you and your loved ones. Everyday take about ten to twenty minutes and just seclude yourself and breath. Go get your nails, or hair done, or just go out to eat alone or with a friend. This is the time to sit and think about who you are and whose you are... You are the Kings kid, fearfully and wonderfully made in the image of Christ. You are blessed and highly favored. You are special and loved by Christ and you are a blessing to anyone and everyone that you know...

Most humble and all wise God, I come interceding for that mother that wife that care- giver that father that provider, that person that has given of themselves for everybody else and don't know how to take care of their own selves, God I'm praying that you would give them strength in every weak area I pray that you would continue to breathe your breath as you give them what they need for this journey and this race. God I pray that you would continue to manifest your glory as only you can that you would regulate their minds and unclog their ears so that they can hear from you and seek you like never before. God I pray for your favor to fall fresh like never before so that in everything that we do, self-care would be first before anything else. I pray that we can be favorable and your sight. God my prayer right now is for new beginnings over every person that will read this book. I thank you in advance in Jesus name I pray Amen Amen and Amen!!!

Prayer Journal

_____

_____

_____

_____

_____

_____

_____

_____

_____

_____

_____

_____

_____

_____

_____

_____

_____

_____

When your Faith is being tried...

James 1:2-4 "Dear brothers and sisters, when troubles of any kind come your way, consider it an opportunity for great joy. For you know that when your faith is tested, your endurance has a chance to grow. So let it grow, for when your endurance is fully developed, you will be perfect and complete, needing nothing."

I believe that just like myself, we all have had those times where we feel like our Faith is being tried. Whenever you come to that place it seems like all hell is breaking loose in your life and it don't seem like God is listening, what do you do???? Keep talking, keep trusting, and keep knowing that God said in **(Hebrews 13:5)** That He will never leave you nor forsake you.

You can't live a life without trials, difficulties, and more reasons to pray. You have to trust and keep God at His word. Beloved the enemy will always try to make you doubt the power, love and compassion that God has. Ask yourself how can He work miracles, and turn things around for you if you don't go through anything? Remember this you can never have a testimony without going through a test.

Most humble and all wise God I come praying for anyone that may be wavering in their faith, God I ask that you would breathe your power in and through each person that need their Faith increased, those that can't hear unclog their ears so that they can listen. Increase their discerning spirit so that they will know when you are speaking. Have your way God in all of us. We need you more and more each day. Hear our humble cries. I thank you in advance for all that you have done, are doing, and will do for your children. We love you Lord on Jesus name I pray Amen Amen and Amen!!!

Prayer Journal

Making room for your gifts...

Proverbs 18:16 "A gift opens the way and ushers the giver into the presence of the great."

We all have at least one gift, whether we know it or not God has gifted each and every one of us with some type of gift to help others as well as ourselves. In this season let's make room for our gifts by removing and deleting those things that keep us in bondage. Those things that will hinder our blessing and steal our joy. No matter if it's a person, place, or thing, if it's stopping you from reaching your full potential in Christ then it's time to release it. Let go and let God. If you hang on to God's promises then you know that your season is now!!!! No matter what distractions may come your way, no matter who tell you that you won't amount to anything, no matter who tries to steal your joy, peace, or your blessings, none of that matters because at the end of the day, God has his hands on you. Just know that you were made for purpose you were brought with a price God loves you and he already knew what you were up against. So on today take a leap of faith and do like Peter and ask God to take your hand as you step out onto the water...

Most humble and all wise God I come today praying for each and every person that do not know what their true gifts are. God I pray that you would manifest your glory like never before, that you would snatch them out of the enemy's hands, God that you will cover them with your blood, Lord as you show us and reveal to us what it is that you have in store for your children, we thank you in advance. Lord I pray that you would make room for each and every one of our gifts that we will be able to walk in our gifts as we walk in victory that we would trust you and do your will God we thank you in advance for removing the naysayers from our presence as you continue to build us up and fill us up like never before I thank you for what's about to take place in Jesus name I pray Amen Amen and Amen!!!!

Prayer Journal

_____

_____

_____

_____

_____

_____

_____

_____

_____

_____

_____

_____

_____

_____

_____

_____

_____

Snatching your children from the enemy's hand...

Psalms 23:1-6 "The Lord is my shepherd, I lack nothing. He makes me lie down in green pastures, he leads me beside quiet waters, he refreshes my soul. He guides me along the right paths for his name's sake. Even though I walk through the darkest valley, I will fear no evil, for you are with me; your rod and your staff, they comfort me. You prepare a table before me in the presence of my enemies. You anoint my head with oil; my cup overflows. Surely your goodness and love will follow me all the days of my life, and I will dwell in the house of the Lord forever."

The enemy has an agenda, his agenda is to steal kill and destroy. In this season he has been focusing on our young people. We have to remember that
Isaiah 59:19 says
So shall they fear the name of the Lord from the west and His glory from the rising of the sun; When the enemy shall come in like a flood, the Spirit of the Lord shall lift up a standard against him...
I know that it can be hard when your child is disrespectful or disobedient, but you have to know that when we give up on our children we are putting them in harm's way. When we are not covering our children we are opening up a foot hole for the enemy to creep in. In this season we have to stand and take our rightful position and know without a shadow of a doubt that we are the kings' kids and if we are God's child that means our children are also. Family stay prayed up, plead the blood over your children. Speak favor over them. Let them know how blessed they are and keep them in the word, especially now in these wicked days that we are living in.

Most humble and all wise God I come praying for that wayward child, Lord I pray that you would snatch them out of the enemy's hand, cover them with your blood. Lead them on a path of righteousness. God I ask that you would strengthen every parent that has endured heartache that has come at the hands of their children. Lord I pray for newness, healing, strength, peace, and deliverance over these families. I ask that you would go through the minds, hearts and the homes of each family like a mighty rushing wind taking total and complete control over every situation. Show up suddenly as only you can. God I thank you in advance for what you are about to do. Amen Amen and Amen!!!

22

Prayer Journal

_____

_____

_____

_____

_____

_____

_____

_____

_____

_____

_____

_____

_____

_____

_____

_____

_____

_____

_____

Recovering after abuse

Psalms 147:3 "He heals the brokenhearted and binds up their wounds."

I told you in the beginning of this book that you would experience some of me in this devotional. I was about five years old when I was molested. I can still remember it like it was yesterday. I did as so many people do; I held it in for years. When I say years I'm talking about close to thirty years. The first person that I shared this with was my husband and then my mother and older sister. I held on to this not realizing that this was taking control of me. This demon had me in bondage pretty much my whole life. It wasn't until I seen a friend going through that I realized that I needed therapy. It was then that I started seeing my issues clearly. I had seen that this bondage had me holding back and rejecting people, love, and affection. Just know that this is a process and things won't change overnight, but it will surely change. Therapy taught me that journaling helps more than you know. So for every person reading this devotional, I need you to know that you are not worthless, whatever happened to you just know that it wasn't your fault, you are not what the enemy says that you are, you are healed, delivered, set free, and worthy of greatness and to be victorious. So after reading this I want you to pick up that journal and pen and start writing, releasing everything that the devil has laid dormant on you and in your life. Take back everything that was stolen and start living a victorious life.

Most Holy and all wise God, I come praying today for victims of molestation. God I'm praying that your healing hands will touch them right where they are even now, I'm praying that you would build them up God and let them know what their worth is, I ask that you will continue to remove those things that are keeping them stuck and in bondage, every demon that has laid dormant upon them I pray that you would release them right now as you give them their freedom back. God give them their joy, peace and everything that was stolen away from them on that day or night that the enemy tried to destroy in them. I pray for you to touch them, cover them, breathed over them, speak to them, use them as mighty vessels guard them, let them know that they have a life to live in that what the enemy met for evil you have turned it around for good so I thank you in advance for guiding and showing up mightily in their lives. Every trick, every scheme, every attack, that the enemy thought he was placing upon them God has intercepted it and that you are taking it away and turning it around. Lord I thank you in advance for healing right now and releasing in the name of Jesus that as they read this God they will feel your peace and your comfort like never before God I thank you in advance for who you are and whose we are in you. God now show up because they need you more today than on yesterday. God I thank you in advance. God you have always covered us and kept us even when we didn't realize it and even when it didn't feel like it so I thank you God because things could have been so much worse now have your way that we will be all that you have called as to be in Jesus name I pray Amen Amen and Amen!!!

Prayer Journal

Being a people pleaser

Galatians 1:10 "Am I now trying to win the approval of human beings, or of God? Or am I trying to please people? If I were still trying to please people, I would not be a servant of Christ."
Galatians 1:10 NIV

My whole life I've been a people pleaser, I'm not sure if it's because of my past or not. I always had this thing where I couldn't stand for anyone to be mad at me, in turn I would rather make myself uncomfortable just for someone else to get what they may want. I never said no even if I was screaming it in side. I never realized how bad it was until someone had given me a book entitled (When pleasing others is hurting you). The title alone had me rethinking my life. Sometimes in life when you have been hurt, abused, or just not feeling loved; you tend to mask your pain by trying to please others. In doing this you think that you are avoiding additional hurt and pain in your life. I'm here to tell you that doing this will never work, it's not until you address your past that you can and will be able to move toward your future. Whatever hurt or pain that has been laying dormant in your life will remain and grow if you don't release it and deal with it. I pray that you would deal with it before it's too late. For me I waited until I had to place an empty chair in place of the person that hurt me as a child and expressed the hurt, pain, and anger towards this person I was able to get my freedom back. DON'T DO WHAT I DID!!!! Don't hold on to the things that tried to destroy you release and be free.

Most precious and all knowing God I come on behalf of that broken boy or girl, man or woman that has been holding on to their past and hindering their future. God I ask that you would unclog their ears and allow them to hear from you. Lord please let any and everyone that picks up this devotional be able feel your presence and anointing as they read it. God I speak release and restoration over every stronghold that has any of us in bondage. Lord heal mind body and soul as only you can. God meet us at our very need. Lord I need for you to take control even if we don't want you to. God in this season allow us to see miracles signs and wonders. Give us the strength that is needed for us to take back everything that was stolen. Our joy, peace, self worth, and strength, God Allow us to know that we are victorious in Jesus name I pray Amen Amen and Amen!!!

Prayer Journal

_____

_____

_____

_____

_____

_____

_____

_____

_____

_____

_____

_____

_____

_____

_____

_____

_____

_____

_____

_____

Taking your life back after the enemy tries to destroy you...

James 4:7 "Submit yourselves, then, to God. Resist the devil, and he will flee from you."

When living a life for Christ the enemy will always try to destroy you and your destiny. I have been serving God for most of my life, and even before I started following and serving Him the enemy has been trying to destroy my Destiny. My life has had its ups and downs and through it all He has always been right there with me. Life comes at you fast, and you may feel like giving up because the enemy is pressing so hard that you don't know how to get relief. The enemy may have taken your choice but not your calling. Let me tell you when it gets this hard it's because the enemy has peeped into your future and sees the power, blessings, and the anointing that is on your life. If he can destroy your Destiny then he will destroy the destiny of all those that you are suppose to bless. In this season we have to stomp on the enemies head and declare that God has already equipped you for this. Just know at the end of the day you WIN!!!

Most humble and all wise God I come praying for your people, Lord I pray for strength to fight this battle. Lord we need you to cover and keep us that the destiny that you have ordained for us will come to pass. Lord we can do nothing without you. We need you to walk with us, talk with us, and keep us. No matter what it looks like, Lord fill us up. Give us a fresh anointing, a fresh wind, we have emptied ourselves and need to be filled with you spirit. We don't want to give up we want to please you in everything that we do. God we want to glorify you and horrify the enemy. Take total and complete control over every situation and attack that comes our way. We thank you in advance. Amen Amen and Amen!!!

Prayer Journal

_____

_____

_____

_____

_____

_____

_____

_____

_____

_____

_____

_____

_____

_____

_____

_____

_____

_____

_____

_____

Holding on to Unforgiveness!!!!

Matthews 6:14-15 "For if you forgive other people when they sin against you, your heavenly Father will also forgive you. But if you do not forgive others their sins, your Father will not forgive your sins."

In life we have all been hurt one time or another. We take that hurt and harbor it and let it fester. What we don't realize is that the enemy will use your hurt to defeat and destroy you. Hurt people hurt people is what they say. We as believers must stand strong in every situation that the enemy will use against us. You must know that forgiveness is not for the other person it's for you. Have you ever seen how whoever you have an issue with, seems so unbothered about the situation? They are living their best life and you're screaming and crying inside. Statistically those that hold on to Unforgiveness are less healthy than those that don't. Do you want to be made well then take this time to forgive? I know firsthand about holding on to Unforgiveness for years. I decided that life is too short, and I want to live a healthy and prosperous life. So I have forgiven every person that has ever hurt me or did me wrong. At the end of the day God is in control and He is true to His word.
Romans 12:19 Beloved, never avenge yourselves, but leave it to the wrath of God, for it is written, "Vengeance is mine I will repay, says the Lord."
So Unforgiveness has to flee in the name of Jesus....

Most humble and all wise God I come praying against that spirit of Unforgiveness. Lord touch the heart, mind, and spirit of each individual that will read this prayer. I pray for a fresh wind to come over each person. Let them know that as forgiveness take place healing begins, let us know that as forgiveness takes place deliverance takes place, let us know that as forgiveness take place freedom takes place, Let us know that as forgiveness take place joy will take place, let us know that when forgiveness take place wholeness takes place. God do a new and miraculous thing in and through the hearts mind and spirit of your people. I thank you in advance in Jesus name I pray Amen Amen and Amen!!!

Prayer Journal

_____

_____

_____

_____

_____

_____

_____

_____

_____

_____

_____

_____

_____

_____

_____

_____

_____

_____

Losing a loved one

Matthew 5:4 "Blessed are those who mourn, for they will be comforted."

It's hard when you lose a loved one especially when it's someone close like a parent. I was fourteen when my grandmother passed away, it was the hardest thing that I had gone through at least I thought. We have all been in this place one time or another, if you haven't praise God that you have never felt that pain. For me I will never forget that feeling that I had when I lost my grandmother as a child or my dad as an adult. My family has a bond like nothing I've seen so to experience the kind of loss that we have could have literally taken me out. But God. The overwhelming emotions that I felt were and are still unexplainable. We as a human race have to know that it is okay to talk about our pain. We cannot allow our emotions to stay bottled up and destroy us from the inside out. Let's break generational curses in this season. Stop believing that counseling is for the weak, it's time for freedom... today make up in your mind that you will live and not die. Freedom comes with releasing yourself from everything that will hold you back. The time is now....

Most humble and all wise God I come praying for freedom, freedom from ourselves, our thoughts, our suffering, our pain, our selfishness, and everything that has kept us from being who we need to be in you. Lord cover us from the things that we aren't aware of, things that will keep us from reaching our fullest potential. Lord I pray for every Man, Woman, boy, or girl that do not know how to ask for help, or trust you enough to take control over every situation. Lord I thank you in advance for new life in Jesus name Amen Amen and Amen!!!

Prayer Journal

When being busy keeps you from being productive...

Ecclesiastes 9:10 "Whatever your hand finds to do, do it with all your might, for in the realm of the dead, where you are going, there is neither working nor planning nor knowledge nor wisdom."

In life we feel like there's always more work to get done, than there is time in a day. So we wake up and hit the floor running. We spend the bulk of our day catering to our spouse, children, jobs and the things of the world, but how much do we cater to God? When we focus more on Christ we won't just be busy we will be productive. We as Christians must start our day with the Master, so that He can direct us and our paths daily. I know that you fill like you have to do everything or take care of everyone every day but I need you to know that you have to take care of you first. First things first start your day by asking God what is it that He wants you to do today, and go from there.

Rom. 12-2

Do not be conformed to this world, but be transformed by the renewal of your mind, that by testing you may discern what is the will of God, what is good and acceptable and perfect.

Let's renew our minds today and become productive people instead of busy people.

Most humble and all wise God I come on behalf of everyone that has a busy mindset and lifestyle. God I ask that you speak to and through them, that you would show us how to be more productive in this world that is filled with so much chaos, confusion and busyness. Lord please help your children to focus on your will and not our will so that we would live a better life. Take total and complete control over each and every one of us. Allow your spirit to fall fresh like never before. I thank you in advance Amen Amen and Amen!!!

Prayer Journal

_____

_____

_____

_____

_____

_____

_____

_____

_____

_____

_____

_____

_____

_____

_____

_____

_____

_____

_____

_____

Dealing with sickness

1Peter 5:7 "Cast all your anxiety on him because he cares for you."

In life no one is exempt from life's situations. You may have some type of sickness, or a loved one may be suffering from a sickness. You watch them or yourself get better or worse, and pray and wait for healing to take place. You begin to stress, worry, or even question God. One thing that I want you to remember is that your attitude determines your altitude. Every situation is a test, and you have to make up in your mind if you are going to pass or fail. Take everything to God in prayer as you hold Him to His word.... He is a God that cannot lie. If He said it that settles it. Never ever think that you are the only person going through this, and if God did it for them he can surely do it for you.

Most humble and all wise God I Come to say thank you for this day God I'm praying for each and every person that will read this page. I ask that you would manifest your glory, God that you will be the healer and the comforter in this time of need. Lord I pray that you would move by your spirit like never before God, take all the fear and doubt away from your children. Lord I plead the blood of Jesus over every negative thought that will try to destroy any person that may be going through any kind of illness today whether it's a physical illness or mental illness whatever it is that the enemy is trying to do to corrupt or destroy God I pray right now that you will cut it at the root and send him back to the pits of hell now move by your spirit as only you can God take total and complete control Lord send your healing angels to cover and surround every person that is reading this prayer God I thank you in advance for hearing and answering my prayers in Jesus name I pray Amen Amen Amen!!!

Prayer Journal

_____

_____

_____

_____

_____

_____

_____

_____

_____

_____

_____

_____

_____

_____

_____

_____

_____

_____

_____

Sticking and Staying

Proverbs 27:17 "As iron sharpens iron, so one person sharpens another."

There will be times in life when you will want to run far away. Run away from people, situations, ministry, and hurt. I need you to always remember that it's easy to run and harder to stay!!!! Anything worth having is worth Fighting for. In life you won't always get your way, people will betray you, lie on you, disrespect you, hurt you, leave you, disappoint you, and turn their backs on you. I want you to know that
Deuteronomy 31:6
 Be strong and courageous. Do not be afraid or terrified because of them, for the Lord your God goes with you; he will never leave you nor forsake you."

So with that being said people are people and Christ is and should be everything to and for you! Don't let situations or people allow you or stop you from being who God has called you to be!

Most humble and all wise God I come praying for every person dealing with hurt of every kind. Lord touch the hearts and minds of each individual so that they may feel you through it all. Lord move through every situation like a mighty rushing wind, showing them that you are in control. God show us how to stick and stay with you through the good and the bad. Lord when the enemy attacks we need you to be our hedge of protection. When we feel all alone be the only one that is needed. God show up like never before in our lives. God we need you to turn things around as only you can. God we know you to be a way maker and a miracle worker, so do a new thing in us. Lord we know that you do all things well, now strengthen us as only you can. Lord we want to be able to be mighty vessels for you but we can't if you don't give us the strength. Have your way in Jesus name Amen Amen and Amen!!!

Prayer Journal

_____

_____

_____

_____

_____

_____

_____

_____

_____

_____

_____

_____

_____

_____

_____

_____

_____

Faith without works is dead...

Hebrews 11:1-3
Faith shows the reality of what we hope for; it is the evidence of things we cannot see. Through their faith, the people in days of old earned a good reputation. By faith we understand that the entire universe was formed at God's command, that what we now see did not come from anything that can be seen.

We as believers pray for God to do things in our lives and expect Him to do it without hesitation. Ask yourself how big is your faith??? Furthermore what are you doing to make sure that this or these things come to pass?
James 2:14 what does it profit, my brethren, if someone says he has faith but does not have works? Can faith save him?
Family it's great to have faith but your actions must accompany that same faith. Don't ask God to bless you with good health and all you do is beat your body or put poison in it daily. Don't ask God to help you to grow in Him but yet you never read your word. This goes for everything that you may be desiring or asking for. The Bible is full of great life changing advice, however we just have to read and absorb it. The Bible is the best teaching tool out there. So as you seek God about life and the changes that you want, make sure that your works coincide with your faith.

Most humble and all wise God I come praying for the body of believers, I pray that you touch each of us with strong faith, Lord help us to make sure that our actions match our faith as well. Jesus I know that you sit high and look low, I'm asking that you help your children to be better in everything thing that we do. Lord touch us and allow us to touch you. God we want faith like the woman with the issue of blood she knew that if she but touched the hem of your garment that she would be made whole. Lord she didn't sit and wait for you to come to her she went to you and showed us how it is done. Now help us Lord to display this kind of faith daily in Jesus name I pray Amen Amen and Amen!!!

Prayer Journal

_____

_____

_____

_____

_____

_____

_____

_____

_____

_____

_____

_____

_____

_____

_____

_____

_____

_____

_____

Not letting the enemy win

Deuteronomy 28:7 "The Lord will grant that the enemies who rise up against you will be defeated before you. They will come at you from one direction but flee from you in seven."

Every day of your life the enemy will try you. His job is to distract and destroy you.
John10:10 The thief comes only to steal and kill and destroy. I came that they may have life and have it abundantly.
No matter what the situation may be you have the power to shut him down. We have to trust God even when we can't trace Him. I know that there have been times in your life where you felt like God wasn't there, those times when you felt like God wasn't there and just like that He showed up in the nick of time.
Hebrew 13:5 Keep your lives free from the love of money and be content with what you have, because God has said, "Never will I leave you; never will I forsake you."
If God said it that settles it. The enemy will always tell you things that will have you doubting yourself and God... just know that the word of God is alive and God speaks to us still to this day through the word.
John 10:27-28
My sheep listen to my voice; I know them, and they follow me. I give them eternal life, and they shall never perish; no one will snatch them out of my hand.
Listen for the voice of God and know that you can conquer and be healed of all things. Past hurts failures, disobedience, and whatever the enemy has laid dormant in your heart and minds....

Most humble and all wise God I come praying for healing over the minds and hearts of every person reading this. God open up ears so that we can hear you clearly and be able to cut off the enemies' voice. Lord remove distractions, fear, and doubt that may arise in us. Take total and complete control over us that we will trust you even when we can't trace you. Move by your spirit as only you can. Use us God as we are willing and able to be used by you. Lord we want to be made whole in the name of Jesus... Amen Amen and Amen!!!

Prayer Journal

_____

_____

_____

_____

_____

_____

_____

_____

_____

_____

_____

_____

_____

_____

_____

_____

_____

_____

Knowing your Worth!!!

Romans 12:2 "Do not conform to the pattern of this world, but be transformed by the renewing of your mind. Then you will be able to test and approve what God's will is—his good, pleasing and perfect will."

When you think about your life you automatically believe that you know your worth, but the truth of the matter is we as a people don't really know our worth. We need to look at our life as doors and we can't let every and anybody come through our door. Just like you keep your doors shut and locked in your physical home, you have to keep the door of your worth shut to people and places that make you feel unworthy. You have to know without a shadow of a doubt you are the Kings kid and you are worthy of nothing but Greatness!!! In this season pray for God to increase your faith that you would believe in yourself and your worth... No longer will you walk in defeat you will walk in victory because God has made you whole. Allow God to transition you as He removes all of the negative thoughts that the enemy has placed in your mind.

Most humble and all wise God I come praying for everyone dealing with worthlessness. Lord heal them mentally in the name of Jesus. God I ask that you would feel them with your strength, wisdom, knowledge and love. Lord speak to them and teach them to know their worth. Help each person not to let the enemy continue to place this spirit of fear over them. Remove every spirit that is not like you in the name of Jesus. Move by your spirit as you take control over every part of them. Lord break down every stronghold that has kept them in bondage and fell them with your precious Holy Spirit in the name of Jesus Amen Amen and Amen!!!

Prayer Journal

Being Broken....

Psalms 34:18 "The Lord is close to the brokenhearted and saves those who are crushed in spirit."

There are days when you may feel like God is nowhere to be found and you are completely broken, that you have no more to give. The enemy wants you to believe that God is nowhere to be found. Not true... the devil will always make you feel like you are losing your mind, that you are done and that it's time to throw in the towel. Let me just tell you that I have been in this place and I know without a shadow of a doubt that God has never left me nor forsaken me. We have to take back what the enemy has stolen and live our best lives. The devil knows your mistakes, your passion and sins. Now it's time for the body of Christ to learn how the enemy work and what he likes. We know that he likes chaos and confusion, and he wants to stick you in the middle if it all. We have the power to turn our situation around. There is power in the name of Jesus and because He has the power we have the power. Speak life over your situation. Stop letting things put you in a box instead put the things that have been holding you back and in bondage in a box, close it and never reopen it again....

Most Holy and all wise God I come praying on behalf of that broken person. That person that feel like life has gotten too hard for them, God I come against that spirit of defeat right now in the name of Jesus, Lord I pray that you would take control of their thought process and everything that the enemy has planted in their minds. God allow these things to be removed in the name of Jesus. I pray that they will stand in take their rightful position in life and know without a shadow of a doubt that they have the power to tell those things to be removed and released from them. God I ask that you would strengthen each and every person reading this that you will continue to have your way like never before. God I thank you in advance for turning things around that you will be glorified in the enemy will be horrified. Show up mightily God that everything that each and every person that's reading this maybe experiencing, brokenness, defeat or just going through, God please touch them right now that they would feel your presence and your anointing. Lord I thank you right now for what's about to take place in and through the lives of each and every person that decided to read this journal God I ask that you would move by your spirit that everything that maybe holding them in bondage is released and lifted up off of them even right now, I thank you God for your love I thank you for always hearing and answering my prayers have your way I will be forever grateful to praise, honor and glorify you in Jesus name I pray Amen Amen and Amen!!!!

Prayer Journal

_____

_____

_____

_____

_____

_____

_____

_____

_____

_____

_____

_____

_____

_____

_____

_____

_____

_____

_____

Leading the youth in a time where everything is Accepted!!!

Romans 6:23 "For the wages of sin is death, but the gift of God is eternal life in Christ Jesus our Lord."

In this season society says that everything is acceptable. You may be struggling with trying to have conversations with your young people, being as though most young people think that they know everything anyways. Raising your children in church you would think that they would focus on what the word says, but peer pressure is real, as well as the desire to sin. We as the body of Christ have to PRAY constantly for our youth because the enemy is always preying on them as he seeks to kill and destroy them. We have to keep putting the word in them... let the word rest in their spirit. We know what the word says and we must trust it with our whole heart. We have to teach our young people that it is okay to love the person and hate the sin. We should never let them believe that sin is okay. In this season we must pray diligently and constantly for our young people. They are our next generation that will take this world by storm, so that mean that we must teach them accordingly. God can do all things but fail and if we trust Him and put Him first we will reap if we faint not...
Proverbs 22:6. Train up a child in the way he should go: and when he is old, he will not depart from it...
That being said keep planting the seeds of Godliness into our young people it is a must...

Most holy and righteous God we come praying that you would speak to our young people, Lord I ask that you would bring back to their remembrance all that was instilled in them. Lord take total control over their mindset. Remove everything that the enemy has tried to lay dormant in them. Allow them to put you first. Lord please touch each parent that has to raise children in this season. Lord give us as parents every word to say that will speak to the young people. Lord touch the Pastor's, Youth Pastors, and advisors that has to speak into our young people. Lord we need you right now. We are living in a season where people have no regard for life we need you to turn it around. Show up God as only you can. Move by your spirit Lord, go through like a mighty rushing wind healing the mindset of your children so that we can live a life that is pleasing unto you... from my mouth to your ears have your way... in Jesus name I pray Amen Amen and Amen!!!

Prayer Journal

_____

_____

_____

_____

_____

_____

_____

_____

_____

_____

_____

_____

_____

_____

_____

_____

_____

_____

_____

When you feel Helpless!!!

Philippians 4:13 "I can do all things through him who gives me strength."

In life you will come up against some things that may have you feeling helpless. That's when you have to remember that when you are weak He is strong!!! God is never helpless and He is in control of everything. He is Alpha and Omega the Beginning and the End...
I know that in times of heartache, struggles, difficulties, and confusion, it's hard to see how Good God really is. Trust me I am you and you are me. I have experienced the ultimate heartache losing both my parents and grandparents has been a struggle for me, but losing my mother could have literally taken me out. I thought that it was hard when my dad passed away, but losing my mother... This woman was everything; she was a great mother, a best friend to her children and grandchildren, and the matriarch of my family. I felt as if God was no longer hearing me because my prayers for her healing hadn't been answered. My faith began to fade, as I began to lose myself in grief or the lack of grief. For me being a leader in ministry you assume that you have to put your emotions aside for the sake of ministry. After my father passed I tried to mask my emotions and cover up my short coming so that I would always look strong for everyone else, for that reason I ended up in therapy for four years. I need you to know that you don't have to cover up or mask your feelings or emotions for the sake of anyone. You must release all emotions for your growth. I know that it's not always easy to let your emotions free, especially when you don't want reality to set in. The time will come and once you start your healing you will be able to grow in life as a whole.

Most humble and all wise God I come to you on behalf of every person that have struggles trusting and believing in their time of suffering, Lord help each of us to grow closer to you and seek you in our time of need. Lord it is not easy to see clearly when our heart has been broken into pieces. Lord if we ever needed you before we need you right now. Show up Mightily in the name of Jesus. Lord we may be in a place where we cannot see light at the end of the tunnel, but I do know that you can turn it around and deliver us. God we need your strength and power, losing anyone is hard but losing someone that you couldn't imagine life without is beyond hard. God know that you're a jealous God and that know can come before you, but you are also that same God that taught us how to love. So we need you to comfort us, wrap us in your arms and give us the strength needed to get through. Lord I thank you in advance for what you are going to do in Jesus name Amen!!!

Prayer Journal

_____

_____

_____

_____

_____

_____

_____

_____

_____

_____

_____

_____

_____

_____

_____

_____

_____

_____

_____

_____

When you feel like you are losing your faith...

Hebrews 11:1 "Now faith is confidence in what we hope for and assurance about what we do not see."

Faith is complete trust or confidence in someone or something.

In life you will experience times when you may not be sure as to how strong your faith is. It may be hard for you to see past your emotions or whatever put you in this place. For me I believe that I've trusted God and had larger than mustard seed faith, from the time that I received Christ. No matter what I prayed I just knew that it was going to be answered in Jesus name. People would call on me to pray for them regularly and the prayers would be answered. When my mother had gotten sick, I prayed and prayed and prayed for total and complete healing and it didn't happen. That's when I started questioning how strong my faith was? I believe with everything in me that she would be healed but we had to lay her to rest. This was the hardest thing that I ever had to do. I started feeling like did God hear me if so why didn't he answer me. I use say to people all the time (you know that I'm Jesus home girl) but at that time I questioned everything. Thank God that He won't let you stay in an unsure place for long that is if you truly have a relationship with Him. Instead of focusing on that fact that He called her home I started thinking about the fact that He allowed us to be with her even in a pandemic. This was definitely a blessing especially, when we have been in a season where you were not allowed to have more than two visitors. God is a Great and merciful God and even when we don't see it He does all things well.

Father in the name of Jesus I come praying for a faithless generation. God I ask that you would blow your breath over this world, so that we could see and hear you in this season. Lord we need you more today than on yesterday. God we are living in a time of suffering, heartache, and confusion and we need you to step in. Lord you said in
Deuteronomy: 31:6 Be strong and courageous. Do not be afraid or terrified because of them, for the Lord your God goes with you; he will never leave you nor forsake you."
But as we look at what is going on in the world and those of us that may be struggling with how strong our faith is in this season, all I can say is if we ever needed you before we need you right now!!!
Lord I come on behalf of every person that may be struggling with their faith in this season. Lord I pray that you would regulate the minds and hearts of your people. Father we need you to strengthen the body of Christ that instead of looking at what's going on in the world we would focus on what we can do in the world. God I ask that you would touch each of us from the top of our heads to the soles of our feet, that we would be mighty soldiers in your army. God we need your strength, wisdom, and knowledge so that we can help those that are lost in the world, just like someone helped us. Have your way Jesus like never before, move by your spirit and take control in Jesus name I pray Amen, Amen, and Amen…

Prayer Journal

When it seems like no one understands you!!!

1Peter 5:7 "Cast all your anxiety on him because he cares for you."

Sometimes in life you feel all alone, like the world is against you and nothing that you do or say appears to be right. You feel like you can't do anything right in the eyes of no one. It's in that moment that you need to call on the Father. The one who made you in His perfect image. People will always find flaws and issues with you, be strong and remember that they didn't create you, save you, heal you, cover you, bless you, keep you, or breathe life into you. Take what people say and do as a grain of salt (meaning view something with skepticism or not to interpret something literally) don't allow the world to dictate who you are or whose you are. Always remember that you are the Kings kid, you are royalty. You are beautifully made in His image. So when you look in the mirror you tell yourself I am never alone, my Father in heaven is always in me and with me, I am fearfully and wonderfully made in the image of Christ. He loves me therefore; I love me and when the world is against me He is for me.

Most humble and all wise God I come on behalf of every person that feels like the world don't understand them or the world is against them. God I ask that you would send your loving power to encamp all around each person. Lord unclog ears so that they can hear from you clearly. Lord open eyes so that they can see what you see in them. God I pray that you would build up each person that has low self-esteem and low self-worth. Lord allow your people to know without a shadow of a doubt that you are the only judge in their lives. Move by your Spirit and rain down on each of us like never before. Allow us to feel your love for us daily and always remember that if you are for us who can be against us. Lord I thank you in advance in Jesus name Amen Amen and Amen!!!

Prayer Journal

You will have Good days and Bad days

James 1:2-5
Consider it pure joy, my brothers, when you are involved in various trials, because you know that the testing of your faith produces endurance.

In life you will experience all sorts of things, you will come up against heartache, sickness, loss of loved ones, disappointments, tragedies just to name a few. Being a believer you will have to learn how to fight and sometimes that means fight for your life. The enemy comes to kill steal and destroy, you have the choice as to whether you will allow him to win or lose. It's okay to have bad days but what's not okay is allowing your bad day to outweigh your good days. When the bad days come, first pray and ask God for strength. Secondly after you have prayed I need you to journal. I need you to write down all of your emotions so that they will be off of you. Last put on the full armor of the Lord.

Ephesians 6:10-17 "Finally, be strong in the Lord and in his mighty power. Put on the full armor of God, so that you can take your stand against the devil's schemes. For our struggle is not against flesh and blood, but against the rulers, against the authorities, against the powers of this dark world and against the spiritual forces of evil in the heavenly realms. Therefore put on the full armor of God, so that when the day of evil comes, you may be able to stand your ground, and after you have done everything, to stand. Stand firm then, with the belt of truth buckled around your waist, with the breastplate of righteousness in place, and with your feet fitted with the readiness that comes from the gospel of peace. In addition to all this, take up the shield of faith, with which you can extinguish all the flaming arrows of the evil one. Take the helmet of salvation and the sword of the Spirit, which is the word of God."
In this season you must be clothed in your armor daily.

First thing in the morning last thing at night you must focus on God and what He needs from us, everything else is secondary. When we as believers, stay clothed in our armor that fight becomes a little easier. The Bible tells us that God is with us, so that means that we are never in this fight alone.

Most humble and all wise God I come praying for your children. Lord I ask that you would help us to always be prepared for whatever fight that comes our way. God I ask that you would grant us the strength that we need in this season. Lord we need you to cover us on this journey called life. We know that we are nothing without you and we can't do anything without you. God I ask that you would help us with our bad days that we would not just sit in them and become weak and weary but we would remain strong in you. Take everything that's keeping us stuck and stagnant and revive us a new. God we want to be ready for the task that you have for us, and we also know that we can't and won't be ready if we aren't equipped or prepared. God please prepare us to be who you have called and entrusted us to be in Jesus name I pray Amen Amen and Amen!!!

Prayer Journal

_____

_____

_____

_____

_____

_____

_____

_____

_____

_____

_____

_____

_____

_____

_____

_____

_____

_____

When life becomes so heavy that you can't Pray!!!

Romans 8:26
Likewise the spirit helps us in our weakness. For we do not know what to pray as we ought, but the spirit himself intercedes for us with groanings too deep for words.

Have you ever gone through a season where life was so hard that you couldn't even open your mouth to pray to God for help? When it seemed as if you lost your voice? In life we will all experience this kind of season. When you find yourself in this place just know that God hears your liquid prayers... He heard your silent tears... He hears your heart... Beloved this may be the hardest season of your life, just know that not only do he hear you He also sees you. You are not alone, this season may take your breath away, inhale/exhale and thank God that you still have breath. When you still have breath in your body just know that He still has plans for you.
Jeremiah 29:11 (For I know the plans I have for you," says the Lord. "They are plans for good and not for disaster, to give you a future and a hope.)

Father in the name of Jesus I come on behalf of every person that may be in a season of silence, a season where they don't know what or how to say what needs to be said. God we need you to hear our hearts and our tears. God comfort as only you can. Lord we need you to take control like never before. God life seems so hard and so unfair at times, please move in and through us during these times as we need you more today than on yesterday, we need your power and your strength. We can't do this without you. Have your way Lord for your children need you I thank you in advance for coming to see about us in Jesus name I pray Amen Amen and Amen!!!

Prayer Journal

_____

_____

_____

_____

_____

_____

_____

_____

_____

_____

_____

_____

_____

_____

_____

_____

_____

_____

Love your parents unconditionally!!!

Ephesians 6:2
Honor your father and your mother." This is the first commandment with a promise.

When we are born our parents are the first persons to know and love us. Our parents are our mouth piece, protector, provider, and our bloodline. Parents are the first to show us how to love. Don't get me wrong not all parents know how to love or show love, but our Father in heaven is love and the bible says in
Exodus 20:12 (Honor your father and your mother, that your days may be long in the land that the LORD your God is giving you.) I've always been told that my family is rare, that most families don't love their family as well as others like your family. I am beyond grateful that God blessed me with parents that not only loved me, but showed me how to love. I've heard so many stories of mother/daughter and father/son relationships that are so bad it brings tears to my eyes. Whatever changes that need to take place I pray that you would turn it over to God and let the Father Take control. In this season we have truly seen that life is short. I pray that the love of God falls fresh on every person reading this page right now in the name of Jesus. I pray that you would make up in your mind that starting today you will love your parents unconditionally no matter what the issue is, the next second isn't promised. Don't let whatever happened in your past dictate your future. Let go and let God!!!

Most powerful and all wise God I come on behalf of every person that has difficulties loving their parents. Lord soften their hearts and move in and through them, Lord go through like a mighty rushing wind as you continue to rebuild relationships. Lord I ask that you would close up every foot hole that the enemy would try to use to destroy families. God I ask that you would speak to the situation and those who are involved in the process. God show your children that we need an agape love towards one another. Because we are human and flesh tends to rise when it should be silent we need you to have your way like never before!!! I thank you in advance in Jesus name I pray Amen!!!

Prayer Journal

_____

_____

_____

_____

_____

_____

_____

_____

_____

_____

_____

_____

_____

_____

_____

_____

_____

_____

_____

Not letting the actions of others affect you!!!

Psalm 37:8
Stop being angry! Turn from your rage! Do not lose your temper it only leads to harm.

In life people won't always treat you the way that you want to be treated, or the way that they want to be treated. You have to recognize and realize who you are and whose you are, then you will understand how you should be treated. We as a people have to first look at how we treat ourselves, that's when we will understand why people treat us with or without respect, love, and kindness. This is the season to take back everything that the enemy has stolen from you. Make up in your mind that today is the day that I start loving and respecting me. No longer will I allow anyone to treat me less than the way that I deserve to be treated. Start speaking life over yourself. Don't allow anyone to take you out of character again. Remember that you are the Kings kid and you represent God in everything that you do. Do what you need to do to learn how to treat yourself good so that others will know how to treat you. Read more scriptures on the love of God, read affirmations, fast, pray, treat yourself like royalty whatever it takes. You deserve goodness, respect, and love from anyone that comes in contact with you...

Most humble and all wise God, I come on behalf of every person that may be struggling with loving themselves. God I ask that you would regulate the minds and hearts of your people that we will know that we are worthy of respect and love from everyone and anyone that comes into our lives. Lord help us to love and respect ourselves first so that we can show others how to treat us. Lord remove everyone from us that refuse to treat us with love, respect, and dignity. God I pray that you would move on our behalf, as your spirit rest within so much that people will see you in us. As you cover us anyone that treat us ungodly will feel convicted whenever they miss treat your children. Your word says vengeance is mine says the Lord I will repay. Help us to not mistreat anyone because of the way that they mistreat us. Help us to live according to your word and love our neighbors as you love us in Jesus name I pray Amen Amen and Amen!!!

Prayer Journal

_____

_____

_____

_____

_____

_____

_____

_____

_____

_____

_____

_____

_____

_____

_____

_____

_____

_____

_____

Your beginning to greatness

Romans 8:28
And we know that God causes everything to work together for the good of those who love God and are called according to the purpose for them.

A wise man told me that when you have experienced your greatest loss your growth will take you to greatness... when I heard that I understood but I didn't understand at the same time. Maybe because of the pain that I was feeling at the time, I just didn't want to understand. As I sit back and think about where I've been and where the Lord want to take me I can't help but feel anything but gratitude. My life from childhood has been a fight. I had the best mother in the world. No she wasn't perfect but she was perfect for us. My mother struggled to raise four children, she couldn't provide the best for us as far as materialistic things but what she did give was the kind of love that people dream of getting from a parent. Because of her love I learned how to love my family, my ministry, and myself. I said all of that to say that losing her was the hardest thing that I've gone through. That pain caused my faith to be shaken, but God... the enemy tried to keep me stuck in my grief but my relationship with God is bigger and stronger than anything. I know that this will not be an easy road and I also know that with God on my side I will be stronger than I've ever been, in ministry and in life. Just know that every situation, every life lesson comes to make you stronger and greater. Don't let the enemy keep you stuck and stagnant. You are here for a purpose and God has a plan, it's up to you whether you walk in it or walk away from it. Make the choice!!!

Most humble and all wise God, I come praying for that man, woman, boy or girl that may be struggling with who they are. That person that's trying to figure out the purpose of their life, Lord unclog their ears so that they can hear from you. God please take the blinders off so that they can see clear. Speak to their heart Lord. Move by your spirit as only you can. God I ask that you would go through the heart, mind and spirit like a mighty rushing wind taking control like never before. Allow us all to know that there is greatness inside of us in Jesus name. Lord we need you to release the powers that you have placed in us so that we can change this world to be a better place, a God filled place. I thank you in advance in Jesus name I pray Amen Amen and Amen!!!

Prayer Journal

_____

_____

_____

_____

_____

_____

_____

_____

_____

_____

_____

_____

_____

_____

_____

_____

_____

_____

Not Being afraid to be free!!!

John 8:36 So if the Son sets you free, you are truly free

Being Free... this is something that we all want and need. The issue is that we allow our flesh to get in the way and let fear set in. It's so easy for us to tell people what needs to be done so that they can be free, and not see that we are afraid of that same freedom. Sometimes we believe that we are free, but in reality that is so far from the truth. This is the season for freedom and release. From this day on let's come together and give all of our fears and doubts over to the Lord. I know for a fact that change can be difficult for most and denial is real. I'm preaching to myself, she's me and I am she... most people never know that they are stuck because it's been going on for years. Let me just tell if you are not living your fullest life you aren't free... Pray this prayer with me

Most precious and all knowing God, I come asking that you would release the spirit of been stuck out of my life, Lord move in and through me, take control of my thoughts, heart, mind, and spirit. God I claim freedom over every situation in my life. Lord I declare and decree that today will be the greatest, I declare and decree that change is here, I declare and decree that today I will walk in victory because of who I am and whose I am, today will be the day of new birth as I walk away from bondage into a life of freedom in Jesus name Amen!!!

Prayer Journal

_____

_____

_____

_____

_____

_____

_____

_____

_____

_____

_____

_____

_____

_____

_____

_____

_____

_____

_____

Made in the USA
Middletown, DE
22 May 2021

40197068R00038